Spirit Led Marriage
Our Journey

Jacques & Toshia Posey

Copyright © 2018 Jacques & Toshia Posey

First Edition.

Publisher: Living With More Publications

Cover Design: Monica Mize

All rights reserved. No part of this publication may be reproduced, stored in a retrieval system or transmitted in any form or by any means without the prior written consent of the Author(s) and Publisher. Exceptions are brief quotations within critical articles and reviews.

This work is based on our true story. Some names have been changed to protect the privacy of those even remotely connected to the story. All song lyrics and titles have been properly cited within the text.

Scriptures were taken from the HOLY BIBLE: Various Versions.

ISBN-13: 978-0-692-07210-3

FORWARD

Commitment, covenant, compromise, and forgiveness are the common factors of every marriage that survived a storm. When a couple wholeheartedly embraces the true essence of what these words mean, their marriage will be more successful than the average marriage, even after the storm. In a world where marriage has become less and less sacred and divorce rather than reconciliation is a more promoted and preferred option, this book challenges married couples to pray, to persevere and to work through their difficulties with their faith. The world needs more books such as this that are being written by persons who are willing to share their story with a level of transparency, honesty and insight that is bound to help transform, deliver, and heal broken people and broken marriages.

Every marriage has challenges. The question is how you respond to it. In Christian marriages, we know that the enemy comes to steal, to kill and to destroy our marriages. It is our responsibility to be proactive so that we can be prepared when the attacks come. In a society of inauthenticity, where many pretend and post who they want to be instead of who they really are and what they have overcome, finding role models and guidance in this area isn't easy. Oftentimes, persons feel and believe they are the only ones in their predicament or facing their issue(s) since very few are willing, courageous and shameless enough to expose themselves and their marital issues. In this book, the Posey's do just that. They allow their life to become an open book. They share very candidly their struggles and how unresolved conflict and unfaithfulness gnawed away at their marriage, which ALMOST ended in divorce. They invite and allow the reader to journey with them as they share their individual perspectives of their marital and blended family challenges, the road to reconciliation and their ultimate victory of a successful marriage.

Many marriages will be salvaged and restored because of this book. The relational issues that a lot of couples face are addressed in such a way that the reader is encouraged, inspired and empowered to face their marital and relational issues with confidence, courage and faith. Real, relevant and revelatory describe this book. This book is for single, engaged, divorced and married individuals. We congratulate you for allowing the Posey's through the Holy Spirit to be your "spiritual covenant" coaches to guide you through the process of forgiveness, reconciliation, healing and restoration and ultimately a Spirit Led Marriage.

>   Bro. Carlton and Rev. Theresa Dunston
>   Divine Destiny and Purpose Ministries
>   Powder Springs, Georgia

SPIRIT LED MARRIAGE

AUTHOR'S CONTACT INFO

Email:
spiritledmarriages@gmail.com

Main Website:
www.spiritledmarriages.com

Facebook:
Spirit Led Marriages

Instagram:
Spirit Led Marriages

Dear Reader,

I commend you for acquiring this book and investing in your marriage or upcoming marriage.

Many marriages are failing and headed to divorce court. This is due to ineffective communication, inability to resolve conflict, adultery, past baggage brought into the marriage as well as un-forgiveness.

Marriage was created by God with the first couple - Adam and Eve. God gave instructions to the husband and wife on the marriage relationship throughout His word. To have good success in marriage, we must follow His instruction.

This book was birthed from the many challenges we endured and overcame in the first seven years of our marriage.

We were following the instruction of the world and after many years it landed us on the cusp of separation - almost divorce. By the intervention of the Holy Spirit and being transformed by the renewing of our mind, with the Word of God, we were able to restore our broken relationship.

We have been given the assignment to share our journey with others, in hopes that their marriages and relationship strongholds will be healed and restored. Not only restored, but made new and bring glory unto God. There are steps to achieve healing in your relationship and the first step begins with you.

If you desire a Spirit led marriage you must first have a Spirit led life.

To have a Spirit led life you must have the Holy Spirit living on the inside of you. To have the Holy Spirit living on the inside of you, you must first confess Christ as your Savior and Lord!

Romans 10: 9-10 (NLT) teaches us - If you openly declare that Jesus is Lord and believe in your heart that God raised Him from the dead, you will be saved. For it is by believing in your heart that you are made right with God, and it is by openly declaring your faith that you are saved.

If you have never confessed Christ as your Lord and Savior, this prayer is for you. If you have previously confessed Christ, but have since removed Him from the pilot seat, this prayer is for you as well in rededication.

If you desire the Holy Spirit, then pray this prayer with us:

Father, I ask You to forgive me of my sins. I admit that I fall short of Your glory, but I believe that Jesus Christ lived, died for my sins, then rose again for me. I accept Him as my Lord and my Savior. Fill me with Your Holy Spirit. I surrender my life to You and the leading of Your Spirit. Thank You, Father, for saving me. In Jesus name, Amen.

Welcome to the body of Christ!

UNRESOLVED CONFLICT

"Do you know where your fights and arguments come from? They come from the selfish desires that war within you." James 4:1 NCV

Conflict is an incompatibility between two or more opinions, principles or interest. This is not to be confused with a disagreement. In marriage, you will experience disagreements or opposing opinions that can be resolved by compromising with one another. In compromising you may have to meet in the middle, allowing each person to have a little of their initial desire met.

Our Journey
Toshia

Jacques and I experienced conflict early in our relationship. After dating for six months, we got engaged. We began the process of preparing to merge our lifestyles, families and households together. This brought some conflict because each of us had our own systematic way of running our day to day lives.

We experienced conflict in areas such as deciding - do we rent an apartment or buy a house? How many bedrooms we would need and who would sleep where?

Believe it or not - this discussion blew up into a full-blown argument.

I remember calling Jacques, asking him to meet me for dinner, to talk. I had already decided that this wasn't going to work.

I felt that in this simple decision, he felt the need to fight on behalf of his children's place in our home. It was as if he thought that I was trying to leave them out. I wanted him to realize that somewhere in his beliefs, he felt he had to stand up for his children against me. I also wanted him to see that he was putting them before me, as his soon to be wife. I wanted him to see that if he felt this way - maybe we needed more time to date. Maybe he needed more time to realize my true intentions toward his children, our pending marriage and ultimately our family. I wanted him to know that my heart was for what would work best for everyone, including all our children.

What Jacques was thinking, was the farthest thought from my mind, but to him - it was very real.

The Holy Spirit revealed to me that his turmoil was a result of the guilt he felt because of the effect the divorce had on his children. It also stemmed from the influence of outside sources, telling him to keep his children first in the process of him getting remarried.

I was empathetic to his feelings because I'd been through a divorce. I dealt with the effects that it had on my own children.

We left the restaurant that day with a decision to proceed with our marriage plans and to purchase a house but the conflict was far from over. The seed of division had already been planted.

Over the next few years, we experienced many disagreements that included decisions regarding our children and blending our families. We also began to experience conflict regarding our family members and the influence they had on our behavior in our marriage.

To be perfectly honest with you - there were many times the Holy Spirit spoke to me during and after an argument. But - because I allowed the seed of division to grow in my heart, I was disobedient to His instructions.

I decided that I was tired of Jacques overlooking my feelings and the division that was growing in our home. I made the decision to stand my ground and argue my point every time we had a disagreement. I was going to point out his flaws in handling various situations in hopes that he would realize them and make the necessary adjustments.

I often prayed that God would work on him and show him the error of his ways.

Jacques, on the other hand, was praying that I would see the error of my own ways and realize that I was not perfect. In my mind – obviously - I had no clue of the error of my own ways or that I wasn't perfect. At least not in this matter.

We were fighting for our own selfish desire to be right. We repeatedly ignored the Holy Spirit speaking to us, to help us resolve our conflicts.

Even in our prayers, we were selfish. I did not pray for God to help me to change. I didn't' pray for God to show me the damage that I caused in the situation. I only prayed for God to work on Jacques and for him to be the man and husband I thought he should be.

I am sharing this with you, hoping that you will realize how easy it is for something that seems simple, to lead to a devastating crack in the foundation of any relationship.

Cracks in the foundation of your relationship can lead to ugly and suspicious behaviors. Cracks can lead to all kind of difficulties including pests that can slip through the crack, lay nests and began to harm the structure of your marriage. This is exactly what happened to us.

Prayer

Before we go to the next chapter, if you know that there is unresolved conflict in your marriage, I would like for you to pray this prayer:

Father God, I come before You today, giving You all the glory, all the honor and all the praise for You are a faithful and loving Father. I admit this day, that I am guilty of selfish prayers towards my spouse. I am guilty of arguing and fighting with my spouse to get what I want for the wrong reasons. I have allowed these selfish desires to cause division in my marriage and I ask for forgiveness in Jesus name. Father, I thank You for Your Holy Spirit living on the inside of me. I submit myself to Your Spirit. Teach, lead and remind me of Your Word when I began to operate in the flesh. Father, Your Word tells me that You are against the proud but give grace to the humble. I give myself to You completely. I stand against the devil and I know that he will flee according to Your Word. In Jesus name I pray, Amen.

COMMUNICATION

"Words satisfy the mind as much as fruit does the stomach; good talk is as gratifying as a good harvest. Words kill, words give life; they're either poison or fruit- you choose. Find a good spouse, you find a good life- and even more: the favor of God!" Proverbs 18:20-22 MSG

I believe that every spouse enters their marriage with the intention to have excellent communication, according to their understanding and ability. There is only one problem with that. Many of us communicate based on what we learned from our childhood, past experiences and from being shaped by the world.

Our Truth
Toshia

Jacques and I were both married before, so it's safe to say that we knew what we were looking for in a mate this time around. The one characteristic that we both agreed on, was that our next and final mate should possess, was excellent communication. We both liked to talk and neither one of us liked the feeling of having to pull information out of someone in a conversation.

From our very first conversation, there was a strong attraction to each other. In fact, that's how our relationship began. Through conversation. You see - we met online. Yahoo personals - to be exact. He sent me a message and I sent him my phone number. I wanted to hear his voice and the way he would respond to my many questions. I wanted to hear if I frustrated him or if he would have to scramble for answers.

We were both so pleased with our conversation that Sunday afternoon. It lasted a smooth eight hours. It was like talking to an old friend and getting caught up on life experiences since we last spoke. We quickly developed a friendship over our many long conversations. Our conversations ranged from childhood to our first marriages, children, careers, future dreams and ambitions, and of course, our relationship with God. Jacques could make me laugh like nobody's business with his stories of growing up in rural Kentucky and Indiana.

We started out with pure intentions of developing a lasting friendship and ultimately had a beautiful courtship. I had read many books on communication, blended families and how to make love last. I felt that I was more than prepared to be in a marriage again. That's why I couldn't understand why we were experiencing so many difficulties. Perhaps, it was because in all of the talking we had done, we hadn't concentrated on a few key areas that could make or break any relationship.

As I shared earlier, there was a seed of division planted in our relationship. Our foundation was cracked, but at the time we really had not realized this.

For six years, we communicated to the best of our ability - in our flesh. The first four years we lived in Atlanta and things gradually changed between us. Something was different. I could feel the weight of our spoken and unspoken communication. We still laughed and had fun together, but when it came to major decisions - at times, we would encounter conflict.

In 2011, we were given the opportunity to relocate to Orlando, Florida. We both thought that moving would be the answer to all of our problems. We figured that we would be happy again. A new city, new home and more money! We were going to live the life!

Our mindset was that God had given us a fresh start. He had, but our vision of a fresh start, was far from our reality. Our troubles had just gone to a new level.

We never thought our transition would be so tough. We began arguing more and about everything. Most times, those arguments would end with me saying - "we should live apart for a while and decide if this is what we really want." Too often, I threatened to go back to Atlanta.

Jacques would often tell me - "I can walk away from everything." Looking back, we were both speaking death over our marriage. We were also hurting each other with our words. When he would say that he could walk away - I took it to mean that he wanted to leave and would eventually walk away from me and my children. When he said it, I would retort with – "you can go. I was good before I met you and I will be good when you are gone!"

I didn't realize how this made him feel or the mindset that it was pushing him into. Although he wouldn't share how my words made him feel, I could see the hurt in his eyes.

We knew that our words were hurting each other, but by this time - we were stuck in a vicious cycle. We really didn't know how to get out of it.

Prayer

I would like for you to stop and truly reflect on the pattern of communication that you have with your spouse. Have you been speaking words that are demeaning, mutilating or causing division? If there is a possibility, let's say this prayer together:

Father God, I come before You, in Jesus name. Thank You for loving me so much, that You do not allow me to stay the same. You continue to remind me of Your Word and show me the areas in my life that I need to renew by Your Holy Spirit. I submit the communication, between my spouse and myself to You. I ask You to forgive me for speaking death over my marriage and for speaking words that tear my spouse down. I ask You to remove all unrighteousness and restore my fellowship with You. Your Word tells me that a soft, gentle and thoughtful answer turn away wrath, but harsh, painful and careless words stir up anger. I turn away from foul talk. I submit my conversation to the leading of Your Holy Spirit. Don't allow me to rest in my wrong doing. I pray that my words will bring healing and unity to my marriage and glory to You, God. Thank You, Father, for hearing my prayer. In Jesus name, Amen.

THE TRUTH IN THE MIDDLE OF A LIE

"…..And you shall know the truth, and the truth shall make you free.' John 8:32 NKJV

Many times we can get caught up in the day to day hustle and bustle of life and not realize that what and how we are living is a lie. Things can become so routine that we forget to live on purpose with purpose. Sometimes we start out with good intentions, yet we make decisions along the way, that are contrary to the very vision we started out to fulfill.

Our Story
Toshia

It was a gorgeous Friday afternoon in March 2013. It was the first weekend to be exact. I was more than ready to get off work and head home. We had planned a night out at the movies and dinner as a family. Orlando was so beautiful during that time of the year. You could literally forget that it was still considered winter and mistake it for full-fledged summer time. I was down to my last two patients and then I could break free.

My phone kept buzzing that afternoon and I couldn't figure out why. All of my friends and family knew that I was at work. I decided to call the number back, considering the fact that we had a son away at college and it could have been about him. I didn't get an answer or a voicemail. *Oh well, it must not have been that important or maybe it was a wrong number.*

As I hurried to the parking garage, my cell phone rang. It was from the same number that had been calling me all afternoon.

As I opened my car door, I answered my phone. "Hello, this Is Toshia!"

"Hello, my name is Vickie. Do you know Terry? The voice on the other end responded.

Now, that's not her real name, of course. This book isn't to expose anyone but to share how real this was for us.

Terry! That's Jacques middle name! The name he went by online! "Yes, I know Jacques. He's my husband!"

"Are you still married to him?" She asked.

"Yes I am. Why are you asking?"

"Because I'm his girlfriend and I've been seeing him for 3 years!" That was her response.

I did not immediately believe her. I knew that there were family members and an ex-spouse that would cause problems for us from time to time. I was leaning towards this conclusion.

I began to ask her questions to determine if it was a prank call or indeed a call from a mistress. She was so eager to get to the purpose of her call that she offered to call "Terry" on three way.

I told her -by all means, go right ahead.

Now, I knew that Jacques was running errands and preparing for our night out. I had just spoken to him before I left work. I quietly held the line as she clicked over to call him. To my amazement, I heard my husband answer the phone! I listened as they began to have what seemed like a lover's spat.

The young lady went on to say, "Well, I have your wife on the phone," using that to get a toe hold on the argument.

I heard Jacques choke and I clearly stated - "I am not going to sit on this phone and listen to my husband argue back and forth with his girlfriend! You all can carry on without me! I've heard all that I needed to hear!"

I felt a pain in my belly and instantly became nauseous. Tears began to stream down my face and I began to cry out to God. Actually - I was screaming! Loudly! WHAT IS GOING ON THAT YOU WOULD LET THIS HAPPEN TO ME?

Meanwhile.....

Jacques

After I picked up the phone and began arguing with Vickie and then heard my wife on the line - reality it hit me like a ton of bricks.

Instantly, devastation set in. I hung up the phone and sat in the car wondering - *why did I respond to the first email three years ago from her?* I sat there pondering how I got to that point in my life.

My girlfriend called back. "Why are you doing this?" I questioned.

She was yelling, "You should have told me you were married!" I could feel her pain through her words. I deceived her and my wife.

I told her that it was not *that* type of relationship.

She laughed and said, "I didn't know. Maybe we can be friends one day." It seemed as if she took pleasure in the destruction and unraveling of my marriage. It was as if she thought the situation was funny.

I told her that would never happen. The conversation was over; I hung up the phone.

Regardless of the things that happened over the years between Toshia and I - having that devastation as my reality, was not worth it!

My mind was racing. I realized that the fulfilment of that relationship was not worth the hurt I'd just caused my wife. As I drove back to our apartment, hoping to get there before Toshia, my mind wandered aimlessly. *How did I get into this situation? Why didn't I just tell the truth?*

I felt like a fake and imposter; like my life was in ruins.

I drove back to the apartment in silence. I was thankful that I arrived before Toshia. I sat in the car as my mind raced back and forth. I didn't know what to say to my wife. I literally cried out to God for help. I asked Him what I had truly done. How could I fix this? There seemed to be no words that could explain what I had done to Toshia, but I had to try.

As I was crying out and praying for God to help me, I saw Toshia pull into the parking lot. I felt heaviness in my chest and aches ran through my body. I approached my wife as she sat in the car. Tears rushed down her face. Each step that I took seemed harder than the last. I could see the look of hurt and devastation in her eyes.

I couldn't deny it any longer. I was exposed for who I had become!

Prayer

Father God, I come humbly before You, asking for forgiveness of my sins. I lay down every lie, every word, thought and deed that goes against my marriage and Your will for my life. Cleanse me of all unrighteousness. Remove anything that is not like You and restore my fellowship with You.

I plead the blood of Jesus over my marriage. Thank You for being faithful and just to hear my prayers. I know that it is because of the blood, that I have a right to answered prayer. From this day forward, I stand in expectation of healing, restoration and a greater walk in Christ Jesus. Your Word says the truth shall make me free and whom the Son sets free, is free indeed. I declare that I am free!

As I move forward, I understand that I can do all things through Christ Jesus, who strengthens me. I can face whatever is before me because Your grace is sufficient. I am a victor - not by power nor by might but by Your Spirit. In Jesus name, I pray, Amen.

BAGGAGE CLAIM: HER TICKET

"And do not be conformed to this world [any longer with its superficial values and customs], but be transformed and progressively changed [as you mature spiritually] by the renewing of your mind [focusing on godly values and ethical attitudes], so that you may prove [for yourselves] what the will of God is, that which is good and acceptable and perfect [in His plan and purpose for you]." Romans 12:2 AMP

Toshia

I can't breathe! I gasp for air! My arms are whaling around! I woke up screaming! Then came the heaviness along with tears streaming down my face. Jacques burst through the bedroom door! The look of pity and shame on his face told me that I had not been dreaming. This was my reality. My husband, who I thought was my ride or die, had a girlfriend - for three years! In a million years, I would have never thought that he would do that to me!
How could he?

I loved him through his stupidity in handling the various concerns in our marriage. I put up with his children disrespecting me, his parents talking against me and disrespecting our home. I lived through the fighting and emotional roller coaster of events with his ex-wife.

Was *this* how Jacques was repaying me for my devotion to him?

I put everyone's feelings, needs and concerns before my own. Feeling utterly destroyed end extremely angry, I prayed and cried out - God, you know all that I've been through with him and, yet you let this man hurt me like this! You brought us together. You said he was my husband. Is this really what I'm going to deal with? SERIOUSLY GOD!

Of course, you can tell I've watched way too much Gray's Anatomy. But seriously, I had been a good wife and mother. Heck, I had been a good sister, friend, daughter and all-around good person!

Why would this happen to me? I always tried to help others, see the best in others and encourage others that they could be their best self.

Through tears of frustration and angry sobs, I yelled at God - WHEN IS SOMEONE GOING TO TAKE CARE OF ME?!

For a solid week and a half, this was my song and dance. I went to class and came home moping and feeling sorry for myself. I blamed everyone else for my current circumstances – yes, even God.

Those who were close to me were privy to what was going on in our home. They knew that at any time, one of us was on the couch and the other was in the bedroom. I smoked 2-3 cigars a day. Not black and mild, but the big premium cigars. I was drinking a half of bottle to a full bottle of wine a day and listening to the sorry, woe is me love songs, such as "On My Own" by Patti Labelle. I learned of these songs from my mom as a child.

I refused to pray even though my friends advised me to do so. For some reason, I just wanted to stay in that place. My spirit was wrestling and tugging at me and I was purposely trying to ignore Him.

One evening, I was in class attempting to listen to the teacher give a lecture. My mind was so far from that classroom, I had forgotten that I was even there. Tears began streaming down my face uncontrollably. My vision was blurred. My heart was twisted with pain. At that moment, all I wanted was a cup of McDonald's coffee and a cigar. I left at the midpoint break and never returned.

In the car - I called and told Jacques that I was withdrawing from class because I just could not focus. Of course, he apologized stating that it was all his fault. Inside, I was saying the same thing and rolling my eyes at the phone. I hurried off the call because I didn't want to hear the apologies anymore. I was sick of everything and everybody!

I left school and headed to McDonald's. I was going through the drive thru crying and long-faced. I quickly dried my face as I approached the window to pay. The young, teenage man greeted me and told me my price. He looked at me and said I looked like I was having a rough day. I gave him the change for my coffee, did a quick shrug and grunt while staring ahead.

As he handed me my coffee, he spoke words of wisdom to me. He said, "no matter what it is that you are going through, if you pray and talk to God about it, He will help you." I turned and stared at him with my head slightly tilted to the side.

At that moment, I felt like the Holy Spirit was talking directly to me through this young man. He didn't know me from Adam, but he helped me in ways he may never know.

I was reminded of God's word. "You have taught children and infants to tell of your strength, silencing your enemies and all who oppose you." Psalms 8:25 NLT

Instantly, I felt ready! I was finally ready to talk to my Father and hear His instruction. Immediately, right there in the car, I started praying! After praying and talking with God, He answered my question – When is someone going to take care of me?

He revealed to me that He has always taken care of me. God had always been there for me, but I didn't recognize Him. He showed me that I was so busy trying to fight my battles, fix my situations and design my life, according to what I knew from the world, that I had not recognized that He had been with me all along.

Even when I thought that I was consulting God - I wasn't. I was merely telling God my plans and informing Him of what I wanted Him to do, to make my plans happen. The Lord also revealed to me that I had placed my husband in a position in my life and heart that only the Lord should dwell. I placed such lofty expectations and needs on him that all he could do was fail. Only my Heavenly Father could fulfill those needs and expectations.

I thought that because God had confirmed to me that Jacques was my husband, that he would never let me down, never hurt me or neglect me like my parents had. I put so much responsibility on him for my happiness, that he could not be himself. He was not free to learn from his mistakes because I didn't give him any room to do so. If he stepped out of line, I was sure to remind him to get back in his place. I was determined that Jacques would be the husband that I had imagined he should be. Unfortunately, all of that was based on my past relationship failures, my parents past failures and what the world said a husband should be to me.

I am not saying that I caused him to cheat on me, but I certainly made it an option.

After having several conversations with the young lady, Jacques and with the Lord - I learned that this relationship was one that gave Jacques an outlet from what was going on with us. She was someone for him to talk to and not have to argue. I found out that they had never been physically intimate although they went on three dates and had kissed three times. I had to know what I was dealing with since this had been going on for three years. That was also important for me to know. Those factors would determine if I was able to proceed in the marriage or not.

The truth is, I did a thorough observation of his faults and actions, but I never saw what I was doing. I only saw what he had done!

My ex-boyfriend had been calling me yearly, sometimes twice a year, to confirm that I was still married. He was keeping tabs on me and feeling out his chances of us getting back together. I would laugh and smile stating that I was still married. I may have even complained a little about my marriage and what was going on, depending on what day he called me. I entertained those calls every time - not once thinking that I was doing anything wrong. I can admit now, that I welcomed them. I enjoyed the attention and even thought from time to time, that Jacques had better get his act together because he had competition.

Wow! How silly does that sound?

This is the man that God brought into my life and I deemed my ex-boyfriend as competition! In the back of my mind, this was like plan C. I was always taught to have a plan A, B, and C if necessary. I knew that this dude would relish the opportunity to be back in a relationship with me.

Ladies, in case you don't know - this is a form of infidelity also. Sometimes we forget why we stopped dating someone when our current relationship is in turmoil. The grass always looks greener on the other side. I've learned that if you mow, fertilize and water your own grass, it can be healthy from the root and green to the eye.

I am forever grateful to the Lord for pursuing me to the point of using a teenager to get my attention. He didn't allow me to rest in ignorance. Instead, God opened my spiritual eyes so that I could see myself for who I had become.

Prayer

If you can relate to anything that was shared here, I'd like to pray with you.

Father God, I come before You laying myself at Your altar. Thank You for Jesus, my High Priest, my Lord and my Savior, the one who is before You on my behalf, interceding. I call You faithful, righteous, loving and just. Thank You for pursuing me daily, not letting me rest in my wrong doing and for drawing me unto You by Your Spirit. Father, I confess my sins in my marriage. I repent for putting my spouse in a place in my life and heart that only You should dwell. I pray that all contaminating communication with anyone outside of my marriage is removed. Purify me and purify my marriage that it may glorify You and draw others to the Kingdom. Father, I confess that my life is not my own but I belong to You. I submit myself to You and to my spouse. I rebuke and cast down every stronghold, thought and past hurt that has been a hindrance in my marriage. I speak peace, joy and unity over my marriage, right now, in the name of Jesus. No weapon formed against me, my spouse or our marriage shall prosper. Father, I welcome Your plan for us and I listen for Your instruction. I submit to Your Word that I may be transformed and progressively changed by the renewing of my mind. I confess that I no longer desire to be conformed to this world, but I desire Your plan and purpose for me. In Jesus name, I pray and thank You Father, Amen.

BAGGAGE CLAIM: HIS TICKET

"The heart is hopelessly dark and deceitful, a puzzle that no one can figure out. But I, God, search the heart and examine the mind. I get to the heart of the human. I get to the root of things. I treat them as they really are, not as they pretend to be." Jeremiah 17:9-10 MSG

Jacques

I came from a household with both parents in the home. My parents have been married for 50 years. Although my parents had been married for a long time, I still didn't understand what marriage was about. My views of marriage and relationships where very cloudy and distorted as it pertained to me.

I grew up in church but didn't hold on to the good teaching that would have impacted my life. Over the years, I accepted the influences of relatives and friends who encouraged sleeping with multiple women. This became the norm in my life.

I remember clearly - God was dealing with me. I was feeling very uneasy about the things that I was doing and the relationships I was participating in.

In marriage, people come into the union with baggage and boy, did I have it. Prior to meeting Toshia, I had been married twice. The first time, I dated a young lady for three years and decided that we might as well get married. On the day of the wedding, I wanted to skip out on the wedding and run away. I didn't because my eldest brother was so excited that it was his duty to take me to the church that he wouldn't leave me alone. I went through with the wedding but the marriage only lasted eight months. We realized that we shouldn't have gotten married. I didn't love her and the only reason that it lasted eight months is that we were in a lease and didn't want to break it.

I learned from this experience that I made a foolish decision. I couldn't even explain why I proposed in the first place. The end result was that we divorced and went our separate ways.

In less than a year, I was back to having physical relationships with various women again. I was still feeling empty and unfulfilled in every area of my life.

Deep down inside – I desired a deeper relationship with God, a healthy relationship with a woman and a good work -life balance. I just didn't know how to obtain it.

I started spending time alone to reflect on my life. Not intentionally, but because my life was in such chaos. I was experiencing financial issues that led to me filing bankruptcy. I was in between jobs and wished I had went back to school to enhance my career.

During that time, I met my second wife. I was introduced to her by a good friend. We dated long distance because we lived in two different states. At the time, I was not looking for a committed relationship, but after three months of dating, we found out that we were expecting a child. I wanted to do the right thing and in an effort to provide a stable environment for our child, I decided that we should get married.

Of course, we had our share of challenges. Finances, communication and intimacy were some of them, especially since we never established a relational foundation. In our eight years of marriage, we had two amazing sons, before we decided to separate and eventually divorced.

From this marriage, I learned that I made unfavorable decisions on my own, involved other people in those decisions and I didn't seek God for his guidance.

After the separation and filing for divorce, I felt like a total mess but was trying to keep my life together. I was a single man again, but now - a father. I thought I had really matured and although my intentions were good - I still felt like a failure.

At that point, I was in my thirties, had accomplished some things, but had been very broken in relationships.

I started seeking God like never before because I was so broken. I desperately needed understanding and guidance. I remember calling a prayer line of a well-known Bishop and asked for prayer for my life. I started reading the bible more and attending bible study during the week. I couldn't go to church on Sundays because I worked a second job.

A few months later, I felt that I was ready to date again. As you know, I met Toshia on an online dating site. We started out talking for many hours and recognized that we had great chemistry. Toshia was a down to earth woman that was easy to talk with and the spirit within her was so great! We started dating and the relationship grew into a great romance and friendship that was very refreshing.

We talked about blending our families before getting married but didn't realize the dynamics of the family structure. After getting married, we started having disagreements regarding raising the children. At the same time, I also had my baggage of baby momma drama. I didn't fully have the dynamics of co-parenting worked out with my ex-wife.

So - if you can imagine - things were like a roller coaster during that time in our lives.

At times, I felt like Toshia didn't understand the relationship that I had with her children, which were also mine now. I loved the kids from the beginning. I knew that being with each other meant that we loved and accepted each other's children as our own.

Toshia and I would argue about many things and she would always say that we should just date but not be married. How do you go back to living separately and dating, after you are already married! We were married! We were not a dating couple! When she would say this it would hurt me tremendously. Over the years, that really played with my mind in regards to failing at marriage again. I started to feel like maybe this wasn't what I was cracked up to be in. I always looked at myself to see what my issues were but due to my selfish nature, I would refuse to deal with them.

I kept hurt inside of me that consisted of past failures and mistakes. In my mind, I still viewed myself as being unable to have a stable relationship that didn't display arguing, fighting and disrespect. I internalized built up frustrations for making bad decisions in my career and relationships. I allowed these issues to guide me instead of the Holy Spirit.

When I think about it, I realize that I had unresolved conflict with myself that I brought into the marriage.

Over the years, Toshia and I continued to argue and fight over anything and everything. I was dealing with the stress of advancing in my career and I was burnt out with what I was experiencing in life.

Toshia and I were not going to church very much nor did we study any Word outside of church attendance. We became focused on hanging out and having a good time in an effort to make things better. We were spiraling out of control but ignored the warning signs that where flashing at us.

I loved Toshia, but just wanted things to go back to the way they were, when we were dating and first married. We had such happy times. She was a great confidante and friend, but things changed quickly.

We continued to have bad arguments time after time. We sought counseling, but because I was not being fully open about my feelings-it still didn't help. I got to a point that I didn't feel like discussing anything due to the nasty fights and arguments that we would have.

One day, I received an email from a woman that I knew prior to meeting Toshia. I responded and started conversing with her. That was the start of a different relationship. It started with an email and led to many phone conversations. At that time, she was someone of the opposite sex, that I could talk to and not have to argue with.

In 2011, I finally had the opportunity to move to Orlando and further my career - so I thought. Toshia and I moved to Orlando and we started a new life. In my mind, I thought that moving to Orlando would stop us from fighting and arguing. I was wrong!

By the time we moved to Orlando, I had become very arrogant and cocky. I felt like my degrees and education were finally paying off. I had a new job, was making more money, and had a new car. I felt like I was living life! I wasn't.

My marriage was still a mess and I was still a mess inside. At that time in my life, I didn't put God in the driver seat. Unfortunately, I made poor, selfish decisions. I was operating in my feelings and the ways of the world.

Over time, I continued the relationship with the woman, having many discussions and meeting up a couple of times. Even though we didn't have sex, it was dead wrong and unnecessary. Throughout that relationship, I felt very uncomfortable and convicted in my actions. I started to come clean about what was going on, but I didn't.

Unfortunately, the day came when it all came out and it changed our lives in a major way.

As I saw my wife, hurt and wounded, I was hit with the reality of what I was really doing. Every moment of our marriage flashed in front of me. I was reminded that I was now another person, along with the other people, who had hurt her. I further damaged what was already fragile.

I would sit and wonder how I got to that place in my life that I would cheat in my marriage. I had no one to blame but myself! I had to own it. I couldn't blame Toshia or anyone else. I had to be accountable and responsible for my own actions. It was at that point that I had to decide to fight for my marriage, *if* she even wanted to stay in it.

Prayer

When you are married, you may go through some ups and downs. It doesn't give you the right to do whatever you want. You must seek God and live according to His Word and experience the transforming of your mind. If I would have done this, I could have handled my marriage better, even during the tough times. If I expected to have a great marriage with Toshia, I had to be the change that needed to be seen. If you can relate to anything that I have shared, let's pray together.

Father in Heaven, thank You for Your love and guidance. Thank You for Your grace and mercy, Father. Lord, I submit my marriage to You and ask You to uncover all hidden sins. Lord, restore and heal the heart of my spouse and myself. Help us to understand the importance of our marriage. Father, let Your Word purify and transform our minds so that we can see the true benefit of being married to each other. Father, I thank You, for your love and hearing my earnest fervent prayer. In Jesus name, Amen.

FORGIVENESS

"For if you forgive other people when they sin against you, your heavenly Father will also forgive you." Matthew 6:14 NIV

"Let me give you a new command: Love one another. In the same way I loved you, you love one another. This is how everyone will recognize that you are my disciples-when they see the love you have for each other." John 13:34-35 MSG

A part of loving your spouse is being able to forgive. Love does not keep a record of being wronged. It doesn't give up on each other. It is always hopeful and endures through every circumstance (1 Corinthians 13). This is the love that Jesus would have us to experience in our marriages and display to the world.

Forgiveness is not an option, it's a mandate. Often, we place restrictions on our desire and ability to forgive. We determine if we will forgive based on the level of the offense or who the offender is. We are also quick to see someone else's sin but not our own. When we forgive others of their sin or offense toward us, we put ourselves in position to be forgiven by our Father. We will all come to a crossroad in our lives where we will need to be forgiven. When our sin is revealed, we must also learn to forgive ourselves and use the lesson to grow in spiritual maturity.

Our Story

After a lot of crying, feeling sorry for ourselves and talking to God, we decided to talk to each other about what we were feeling. After talking with God and finally understanding our roles in the down fall of our marriage, there was a calm and certain peace that was between us.

We started talking with a Christian counselor, or should I say, went back to the Christian counselor that we had only completed a series of sessions with. Yes - we were actually in counseling during the time that both of us were communicating with someone outside of our marriage. No - neither one of us admitted to outside relationships in our joint sessions or our individual sessions.

Toshia

I remember telling our counselor that something was not right with Jacques. I felt that he was seeing someone else. She would insist that she had talked to him and he loved me. She said it was simply in my mind. Of course, I never mentioned my ex-boyfriend either because remember - I didn't think I was doing anything wrong.

When we went back to counseling, we began to talk openly about all the issues that had plagued our marriage. We continued our open dialogue during the time set aside for our homework. We discussed how we had allowed our children to be out of place in our marriage.

I know a lot of people will not agree but the children should not come before your spouse, even in a blended family. Also, they should not come before your relationship with God.

We had to discuss how family members and ex-spouses had been allowed to cause tension in our relationship. This tension continued to build and eventually crossed over into disrespect.

We allowed each other to talk and we actively listened to each other. We truly listened to understand and empathize with the other. I realized how hurtful it was to Jacques whenever I reminded him of his failures and bad decisions. It also caused him to become bewildered.

Ladies, I know that you believe you will feel better if you just tell your husband off sometimes. When I say tell him off - I mean laying it all out and telling him how things are just not working because of HIM. I **strongly** urge you to avoid this behavior. It does not work in your favor. This was Jacques' greatest issue and challenge with me in our marriage.

I, on the other hand, felt as though everyone else's feelings were more important to him than mine. I felt like I was in fourth place in his life eighty percent of the time. I know that you are wondering – eighty percent, Toshia! Yes, eighty percent was the number that I attached to my feelings. It was like I was only a priority for him when we went on vacation, since we were usually out of the country. Because of that, we did not use our phone or talk with anyone at home during that time. That was the only time we truly focused on each other.

I don't know about you, but I don't want to fight for a place in my husband's life. Not that I am needy and emotionally dependent on him, but I believe that the spouse comes under God, then the children should be both of our priority. This was my greatest issue and challenge in our marriage.

We began laying out all our issues in the marriage - in love. It wasn't to be argumentative but to come to a resolution that was liberating. That was a major change! Through this process, I could hear the Holy Spirit saying to me, "love covers a multitude of sins." 1 Peter 4:8 NLT

It was a time for each of us to recognize the issues, ask God for forgiveness, forgive each other, forgive ourselves and focus on the solution. That's exactly what we did!

Prayer

If you have a situation that is causing division in your marriage or that your spouse is constantly complaining about, let's pray together.

Father God, I come today, laying before You my hurts, disappointments and regrets. I confess my wrongdoing, the confusion I caused and the division that I promoted in my marriage. Father, I ask You to forgive me, as I also forgive my spouse. Reveal to each of us, the concerns of the other, and make us open to receive and make the necessary changes in ourselves.

I realize that my fight is not against flesh and blood and my spouse is not the enemy. My fight is against evil rulers and authorities of the unseen world, against mighty powers in this dark world, and against evil spirits in the heavenly places. I plead the blood of Jesus over my marriage, over myself, my spouse and our household. I speak life into my marriage. Your Word tells me that Jesus came that we might have life and have it more abundantly.

Thank You, Lord - I don't have to live and feel stuck in my marriage but we can love each other according to Your Word. We can be quick to forgive and allow each other space to be corrected by Your Spirit and become more spiritually mature. Thank You, Father, for reminding me that love covers a multitude of sins. I pray that I am led by Your Spirit as I encounter every situation in our marriage. I pray that I glorify You with my actions. Father, make my marriage a marriage that draws others into the Kingdom. In Jesus name, I pray, Amen.

A NEW BEGINNING

"Forget about what's happened; don't keep going over old history. Be alert, be present. I'm about to do something brand-new. It's bursting out! Don't you see it? There it is! I'm making a road through the desert, rivers in the badlands." Isaiah 43:18-19 MSG

After having a major setback in your marriage, it is not uncommon to ask the question - "Where do we go from here?" We asked the same question. It was as if Jesus said, I'm glad you asked! We caution you - be ready when God answers this question for you! It will take dedication, focus, strength and humility. But, be of good cheer. You don't have to go at it alone.

"Two people are better than one, for they can help each other succeed. If one person falls, the other can reach out and help. But someone that falls alone is in real trouble. Likewise, two people lying close together can keep each other warm. But how can one be warm alone? A person standing alone can be attacked and defeated, but two can stand back-to-back and conquer. Three are even better, for a triple-braided cord is not easily broken." Ecclesiastes 49-12 NLT

We encourage you to allow the Holy Spirit to be the third person in your marriage, securing the strength of your union.

Our Story

We confessed that we still loved each other. Despite what we experienced and our previous confessions of possible separation, we realized that we desperately wanted to stay together and for our marriage to be restored. Not only did we desire to be restored, we desired something new, something greater. We wanted a marriage that glorified God.

We realized that for this to happen, we had to make some fundamental changes. If you remember, we were in Orlando and had not been consistent with going to church or surrounding ourselves with other believers. Most importantly, we had not been cultivating our relationship with Jesus Christ.

Our first step was to repent of our sinful lifestyle and rededicate our lives to Christ. Individually, we realized the need to do so and had the desire to have our relationship with Father God in right standing. We knew that we had long ago removed Jesus as Lord of our lives. Actually, let's correct that - when we reflected on our lives, we never allowed Jesus to be Lord of our lives. We had been living a religious life on the fence.

Our second step was to rededicate ourselves to the marriage. To be affective in this process, we had to set some boundaries. Jacques knew that he had to earn my trust back. My request was that he would be open about his feelings. If we had a disagreement, instead of going along with what I wanted, I needed him to speak what the

Holy Spirit was leading him to say and do.

We agreed that if we disagreed - he would have the final say as the head of our home. If things didn't work out as planned, we would trust God and not play the blame game.

One of my request to Jacques, was that he would leave the ringer on his phone turned on and the phone unlocked. Before this point, his phone would be locked whenever he was around me. Also, at any time, until I was comfortable, I could request to look at, answer or use his phone.

Jacques requested that I watch my tone when I spoke to him. He also stated that he would correct me, when he felt that I was getting flip at the mouth or showed any type of disrespect. I agreed to the correction.

The most important boundary or should I say - declaration - was that we were NEVER again to say anything about separation or divorce. We committed that whatever the situation, we would work through it, with the Holy Spirit being our guide. PERIOD!

In our third step, Jacques committed to become a Kingdom man. I committed to become a Kingdom woman. Together, we committed to become a Kingdom couple! You may be asking – Kingdom? What does that mean? I'm glad you asked!

The foundation for this commitment is Matthew 6:30-34 "If God gives such attention to the appearance of wildflowers - most of which are never even seen - don't you think he'll attend to you, take pride in you, and do his best for you? What I'm trying to do here is to get you to relax, to not be so preoccupied with getting, so you can respond to God's giving. People who don't know God and the way he works fuss over these things, but you know both God and how he works. Steep your life in God-reality, God-initiative, and God-provisions. Don't worry about missing out. You'll find all your everyday human concerns will be met. Give your entire attention to what God is doing right now, and don't get worked up about what may or may not happen tomorrow. God will help you deal with whatever hard things come up when the time comes." MSG

We stood on the truth of the word of God concerning us individually and as a couple. We declared that we would seek the Kingdom of God first, truly saturate (steep) ourselves in His word and know that all that we need - He will provide and all that comes our way - He will bring us through.

We realized that we don't have to figure it out. Our Lord is in control of our lives. Before we yielded to God, we would always try to fix things or figure out what to do. We learned to pray, listen for the voice of God and then move when He said move and how He said to move. We became reliant on Him. That brought us together and helped to sustain us in our obedience to Him.

Our fourth step was to bring true intimacy into our relationship. We committed to date nights again so that we'd have time to focus and indulge ourselves in each other. We developed a friendship early on, but we really didn't take the time to understand how the other processed information and situations. This was helpful in being sympathetic and empathetic with one another. Despite what we were faced with, we became confident in each other's desire to work together. We built a rapport that would carry us through the rough patches. We absolutely did not withhold lovemaking as a form of punishment. Because of these changes, our intimate relationship is greater than it ever was in the past.

This process was painful. We had to renew our minds concerning a lot of relationship strongholds. Through the pain and self-denial, we, through God, birthed an amazing bond, relationship, and marriage. A Spirit Led Marriage!

Prayer

Father, I come before You in Jesus name. I repent of any sinful life style that I have led that has caused any division and/or hardship on my marriage and in my relationship with You. Cleanse me of all unrighteousness and restore my fellowship with You. Father, I desire Your plan for me and my marriage. I ask You to do a new thing in me. Give me a desire to have a deeper relationship with Christ. I surrender my life and all that I am to You, Lord. I make You Lord of my life. Father, I surrender my marriage to You. I declare that the Holy Spirit is the third strand in my marriage and I believe that my marriage is not easily broken, starting right now, according to Your

Word. Father, lead us in setting health boundaries that will promote growth in our relationship, as well as a level intimacy that can only be achieved in Christ. I trust Your Word in Matthew 6:30-34 that says I don't need to worry about every little need in my life and marriage, but if I seek the Kingdom of God first, you will give me everything that I need. I declare that my marriage is restored, You are doing a new thing in it and all of our needs are met. I decree that we have a Spirit led marriage in Jesus name, Amen.

EPILOGUE

Our marriage transformation took a year and a half as we worked through the process. God cleaned us up individually, strengthened us collectively and prepared us mentally for the faith fight that was ahead of us as we transitioned back to Atlanta. We decided that our new beginning was worth renewing our vows, especially since we had experienced a supernatural understanding of them. Toshia and I have a deeper respect and love for one another. We are sensitive of each other's feelings and communicate more effectively than before. Today, we are working in ministry together and enjoying the blessings that God has given us.

Any couple that desires to renew and redefine their marriage should remember that there are a few things that need to occur. First, develop and strengthen your faith in God and trust Him. Next, allow the Holy Spirit to be your counselor and mediator during the storms in the marriage. Lastly, keep the Lord as the pilot in all areas of your life. He will make every decision for you, just listen and obey. It is the decision to change that makes the difference, but the decision to let the Spirit lead you in everything is the key!

These lessons in life have shaped our marriage. Through these lessons, we learned that in life you will always be in transition.

ABOUT THE AUTHORS

Jacques and Toshia Posey have been married for eleven years and currently reside in the Atlanta area. They have five amazing young men that range from age fourteen to twenty eight years old. They also have three charming grandsons whom they adore.

Being led by the Holy Spirit, Jacques and Toshia founded Spirit Led Marriages. Their vision and mission is to empower men, women, and couples to understand, embrace and implement how to live a transformed life by the renewing of their mind; especially concerning their relationships and marriages.

Jacques & Toshia Posey

www.ingramcontent.com/pod-product-compliance
Lightning Source LLC
Chambersburg PA
CBHW072037060426
42449CB00010BA/2317